For Zoe, who visited us for a short while,
exemplifying unconditional love.

DADDY FIXES EVERYTHING

Written by Ronen Divon
Illustrated by Annalisa Premoli

New York | London

"Daddy," says Guy, "A wheel fell off my race car."
"Don't worry," says dad. "Daddy will fix it."

"Daddy, my doll's arm came off.
It's Dina, my favorite doll," weeps Karin.

"It's okay," says dad. "Daddy will stitch it."

"Daddy, the coloring page I printed from the computer got torn," sighs Eytan.

"No sweat," says dad. "Daddy will put it back together."

"The light went out in the bathroom," says mom.

← mummy

And dad is already on his way to replace the bulb.

Daddy fixes everything. He
glues, puts screws and hooks.
He reconstructs, puts together
and sets up.

Daddy fixes everything, even
when it's really late. And
what daddy didn't fix today,
he will surely fix tomorrow.

"Daddy, Oggie the hamster's cage door is squeaking," says Danielle.
"Yes, I can hear," says dad. "Daddy will oil it shortly."

"Daddy, Guy broke my space rocket," cries Eytan.
"It's not true," answers Guy, "It broke all by itself."

"I want my space rocket now," demands Eytan.

"Now, now, now, now!"

"Okay, okay..." answers dad. "Daddy will even fly to the moon to fix it."

Daddy fixes everything.
He reconnects, he adds oil,
and he even climbs a ladder
to the sky.
Daddy fixes everything,
if not right now and not
tomorrow then on the day
after tomorrow for sure.

"Daddy, come and see what happened,"
says Danielle.   "What?" asks dad.
"Look at Oggie, he isn't moving,"
whispers Danielle.
"Not moving?" asks dad, "Maybe he is asleep?"
"No, he is not asleep. I called him to come
and eat, I touched him, and he is not
moving." "Are you sure?" asks dad.
"Yes dad, come here and see.
And please fix it quickly."

Daddy comes.
And he sees that Oggie the hamster is indeed not moving.
Oggie, who was with us for so long, is lying on his side.
Our Oggie is not blinking, nor twitching his whiskers.
Oggie is not breathing.

"I am afraid Oggie is no longer with us," says dad.

"What do you mean 'no longer with us'? asks Danielle. "He is right here. Please dad, fix it right away."

"His body is still here," says dad, "but Oggie is no longer in his body. He is dead."

"What do you mean 'dead'?
asks Danielle.
"You can fix him, can't you?"

"No Danielle, this is
something daddy can't fix."
answers dad quietly.

"But daddy fixes everything!"

insists Danielle,

"Everything, everything!"

"Almost everything..."
replies dad.

"No! Not almost! Daddy fixes EVERYTHING – daddy will fix Oggie!"

Danielle shouts.
And she wipes away a tear.

Karin, Guy and Eytan run into the room.

"Oggie is dead, but it's okay," says Danielle.
"Daddy is about to fix him."   She plans the rescue.

"Guy, you go bring daddy some glue,

Eytan, go find a screwdriver.

Karin, hurry and bring a needle and a thread."

"I will bring Oggie a blanket so he won't be cold."

"Children," says dad,

"Oggie is dead. This is something daddy really can't fix."

Hush. Silence.

"We will give Oggie a funeral and bury him by the orange tree," says daddy.

"What's a funny-ral?" asks Guy.
"Why can't you fix it?"

"There are things even daddy cannot fix," explains dad.

"When a soul leaves a body, even a tiny body like Oggie's, We can't bring it back," says dad.

"A fu-ner-al is when we help someone who dies go to rest."

"What is a soul?" asks Karin.

"Why can't we bring Oggie back?" asks Guy.

"Where does the soul go?" asks Eytan.

"And why did it leave at the first place?" asks Danielle.

Daddy can't fix everything.

Daddy can't even answer all the questions.

But he can try.

"A soul is something that you do not see but you may feel in your heart.

Before Oggie was born, and before a baby is born, the soul wears a body

Much like you dress up in the morning.

And much like you undress in the evening,
the soul leaves the body, when it's time to leave.

It's called death.

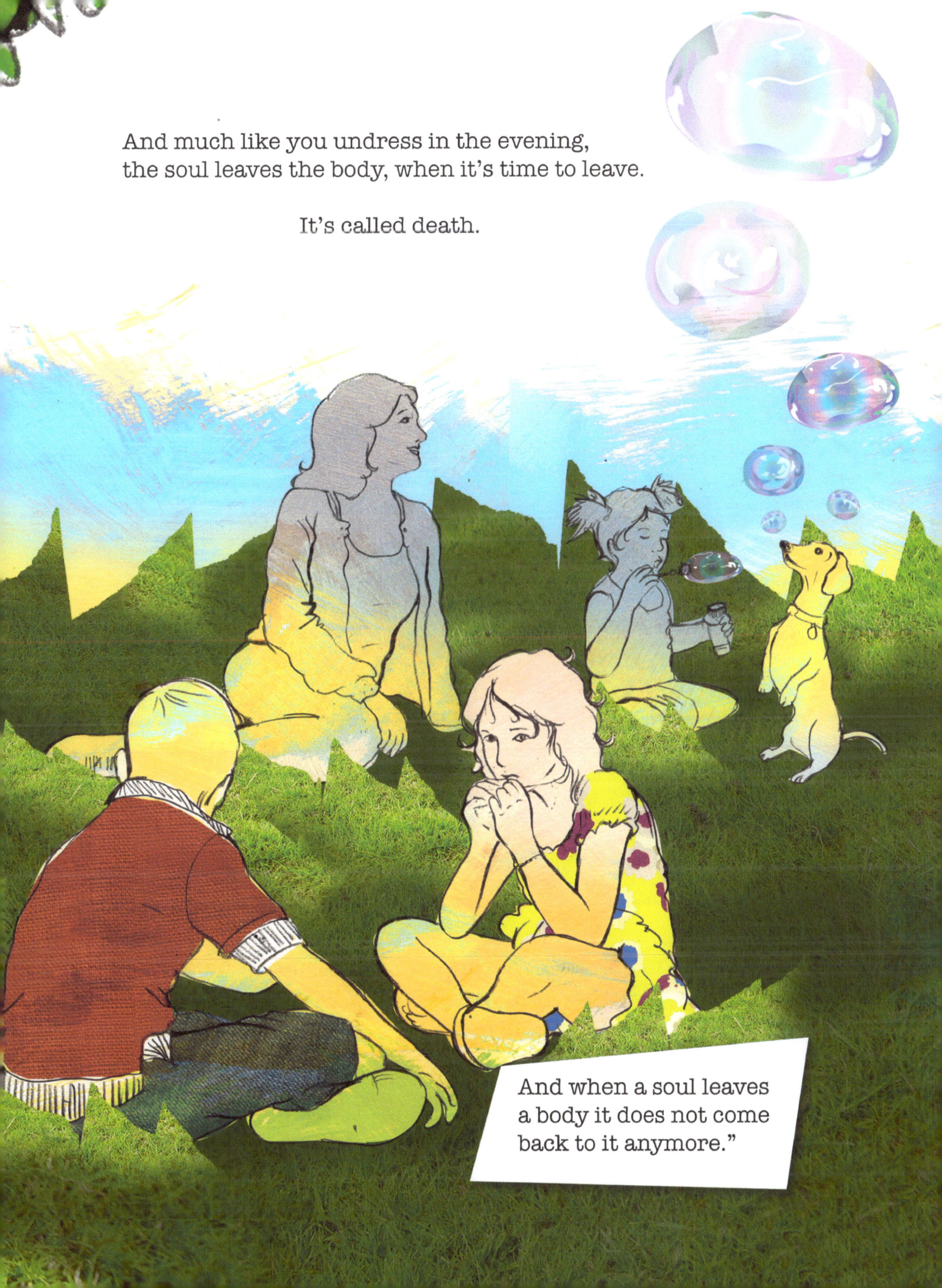

And when a soul leaves
a body it does not come
back to it anymore."

"But where does this soul go?" asks Danielle.

And daddy thinks for a moment and replies: "I'm not sure where the soul goes. There are a lot of answers to this question. You may hear different answers from different people.

But here is one answer: The soul leaves the body when it's time to leave.

"Much like the moment when the day says farewell to the setting sun.

Much like the time when the cloud releases rain.

Much like the day when a chick says goodbye to its parents and flies away from the nest.

Much like the evening when you say goodnight to mom and dad and your brothers and sisters."

Guy, Danielle, Karin and Eytan listen carefully to dad. Karin and Guy wipe away a tear. "It is okay to be sad when someone you love leaves his body," whispers dad. "It is okay to cry, but try to remember that each death is also a new beginning."

"When a chick leaves the nest, she is no longer with her mom and dad. She is starting a new life somewhere else and she is very happy."

"When the day says farewell to the sun, a starry night begins. And when the night is over, morning comes and a new sunrise."

" When a cloud releases rain, water helps plants and vegetables to grow. And that gives us food and water."

"And so it is with Oggie's soul.
It parted ways with us to make
a new beginning."

"Maybe Oggie's soul will come
back to us as a butterfly,
maybe as a flower.

"Maybe Oggie's soul will find a new
world we don't even know about."

"But Oggie is already part of us all.
The memories of the time we all
spent together will never leave us.

And our love for him
will always be there."

So daddy cannot fix everything. But daddy can explain and hug and wipe a tear.
And promise that tomorrow everything will be a little better.

"And so," dad says, "When you think about Oggie or a person who has died... Close your eyes and feel deep inside your heart.

"Then open your eyes, look carefully around you And discover him or her in one of the beautiful things around you."

Guy, Danielle, Karin and Eytan close their eyes tight.

"I see Oggie in the rainbow behind the cloud," says Karin.

"I hear Oggie's squeaking in the music on the radio," says Guy.

"I smell Oggie in the lettuce leafs he loved so much," says Eytan.

"And I feel him deep, deep inside my heart,"
says Danielle.

Special Thanks to my children and wife – a source of constant inspiration,
to Shlomo Abramovih, Annalisa Premoli, Mark Rivlin,
Smadar Katz, Nirit Yona, and many others whose contributions,
direct or indirect, carved this story into being.

www.ingramcontent.com/pod-product-compliance
Lightning Source LLC
LaVergne TN
LVHW072121070426
835511LV00002B/56